AUSTRALIAN

GOURMET
TRAVELLER

chocolate

ACPbooks

contents

chocolate

Little wonder the Spanish tried to keep chocolate to themselves. After bringing it back from their New World colonies in the 16th century, they sweetened it with sugar, added cinnamon and vanilla to further enhance its divine flavour, then promptly monopolised this delicious substance for the next 100 years. Luckily, their ploy didn't work – chocolate was destined to melt its way across borders, continents and oceans to become one of the world's most adored foodstuffs. Dense, rich, complex and utterly satisfying, who can truly say they don't love chocolate? At *Australian Gourmet Traveller*, we find that recipes using chocolate are among those most frequently requested by readers. From sticky cakes and pastries, voluptuous mousses, tarts and ice-creams, to silky-smooth truffles, soothing drinks and meltingly tender biscuits, the demand for more inventive ways to prepare this 'food of the gods' never wanes. So we are very pleased to bring you this special collection of *Australian Gourmet Traveller* chocolate recipes, each one meticulously tested by our expert food team. We're sure that you will enjoy using this book and sharing the luscious results with family and friends – unlike the Spanish, we feel these recipes are too good to keep to ourselves.

Chocolate, espresso and hazelnut pavlova

Soft butter, for greasing
6 egg whites
330g (1½ cups) caster sugar
1½ teaspoons white wine vinegar
1½ teaspoons vanilla extract
2 tablespoons cocoa, sifted
300ml pouring cream
2 tablespoons icing sugar, sifted
2 tablespoons freshly brewed espresso coffee, cooled
200g roasted peeled hazelnuts, coarsely chopped
Icing sugar, optional, for dusting

Preheat oven to 200C. Line an oven tray with foil, mark a 23cm circle onto the foil and lightly grease the circle.

Using an electric mixer, whisk egg whites with a pinch of salt until soft peaks form, then gradually add caster sugar, whisking well after each addition. Continue whisking until all the sugar is added and the mixture is thick and glossy, then whisk in vinegar, vanilla and cocoa until just combined. Spread two-thirds of meringue mixture evenly over the circle, then spoon remaining meringue around edge of circle, forming a rim. Reduce oven temperature to 100C, bake pavlova for 90 minutes, then turn off oven and leave pavlova to cool in oven.

Using an electric mixer, whisk cream and icing sugar until soft peaks form, gently fold in cooled coffee until just combined, then spread mixture over pavlova. Sprinkle pavlova with hazelnuts and dust with icing sugar, if using. Pavlova is best served on day of making.
Serves 8

Sticky chocolate cakes with caramel muscat cream

180g fresh dates, pitted and chopped

85g (½ cup) pitted prunes, chopped

1 teaspoon bicarbonate of soda

75g soft unsalted butter, plus extra, for greasing

150g (¾ cup, firmly packed) brown sugar

2 eggs

150g (1 cup) self-raising flour

120g dark couverture chocolate,
  chopped and refrigerated for 1 hour

Caramel muscat cream

220g (1 cup) caster sugar

40g soft unsalted butter

1 cup pouring cream

300g mascarpone

2 tablespoons liqueur muscat

Combine dates, prunes and 300ml water in a small saucepan and bring just to the boil, then stir in bicarbonate of soda. Process date mixture in a food processor until smooth.

Using an electric mixer, beat butter and sugar until light and fluffy, then add eggs, one at a time, beating well after each. Stir in warm date mixture and flour and mix until well combined. Add chilled chocolate and stir until just incorporated. Divide mixture among 10 greased 125ml dariole moulds or holes of muffin tins and place on an oven tray.

Bake at 170C for 25-35 minutes or until a cake tester withdraws with moist crumbs attached. Stand cakes for 10 minutes, then turn out onto a wire rack, invert onto a plate and cool.

Meanwhile, for caramel muscat cream, combine sugar and ¼ cup boiling water in a small saucepan and stir over low heat until sugar dissolves. Cover and simmer for 3 minutes, then remove lid and boil without stirring until syrup turns a dark caramel colour. Remove from heat and immediately stir in butter and ⅓ cup cream (taking care as mixture will spit), until well combined, then cool slightly. Split cakes, then, using a pastry brush, thickly coat tops of cakes with caramel. Cool remaining caramel to room temperature.

Combine remaining cream, mascarpone, muscat and caramel and whisk until mixture just thickens.

Place small spoonfuls of caramel muscat cream over bottom halves of cakes and replace tops. Serve with remaining caramel muscat cream passed separately.
Makes 10 small cakes

Fig and chocolate bread pudding

100g dried figs, quartered
40g soft unsalted butter
1 loaf of brioche (about 25cm long),
    cut into fifteen 6-8mm-thick slices
100g dark couverture
    chocolate, chopped
220g (1 cup) caster sugar
4 eggs
2 egg yolks
1¼ cups milk
1½ cups pouring cream
Scraped seeds of 1 vanilla bean
Pouring cream, optional, to serve

Place figs in a heatproof bowl, add enough boiling water to cover and stand for 10 minutes, then drain well.

Butter brioche slices on one side, then stand 7-8 slices, slightly overlapping, around edge of a greased 22cm round cake tin, buttered-side facing in. Place 3 slices of brioche, buttered-side up, over base of tin and sprinkle with half the drained figs and half the chocolate, tucking in pieces around overlapping brioche slices. Halve 4 slices of brioche and arrange in centre of pan in a flower pattern, then scatter with remaining figs and chocolate.

Combine sugar, eggs and yolks in a large bowl and whisk until well combined. Add milk, cream and vanilla bean seeds and whisk until well combined, then pour mixture over brioche and stand for 30 minutes for brioche to absorb some of the liquid. Place cake tin in a large roasting pan, add enough boiling water to come halfway up side of tin, then bake at 180C for 30-40 minutes or until just set. Remove tin from water bath and stand for 10 minutes. Serve pudding warm or at room temperature with pouring cream passed separately, if using.

Serves 8

Mexican chocolate pots

1½ cups milk
1 cup pouring cream
2 tablespoons Dutch-process cocoa
200g Mexican-style chocolate, chopped
6 egg yolks

Combine milk and pouring cream in a heavy-based saucepan and bring almost to the boil. Add cocoa and chopped chocolate and whisk until chocolate melts and mixture is smooth.

Place egg yolks in a bowl and gradually whisk in 1 cup chocolate mixture, then whisk in remaining chocolate mixture until combined and strain through a fine sieve into a jug. Divide mixture among six 150ml ramekins or small dishes. Place ramekins in a roasting pan and add enough boiling water to come halfway up sides of ramekins, then cover loosely with foil, pierce foil to allow steam to escape and bake at 150C for 40-45 minutes or until just set. Refrigerate for 4 hours or overnight before serving.
Serves 6

Torrone molle

60g currants

50ml Amaretto, brandy or orange-flavoured liqueur

300g dark couverture chocolate, finely chopped

200g unsalted butter, chopped

2 eggs

100g caster sugar

100g amaretti biscuits, coarsely crushed

125g digestive, shortbread or other un-iced
   biscuits, coarsely crushed

125g glacé citron or glacé orange,
   or a combination of both, chopped

50g ready-soaked figs, stems removed, chopped

60g blanched whole almonds,
   roasted and coarsely chopped

Combine currants and liqueur in a small bowl and stand for 1 hour.

Melt chocolate and butter in a heatproof bowl over a saucepan of simmering water and stir until smooth. Whisk eggs and sugar in a bowl until mixture is thick and holds a trail, then stir into chocolate mixture with currant mixture and remaining ingredients.

Rinse a 1-litre milk carton and dry, spoon in chocolate mixture, tap on a work surface to release any air pockets, then staple top of carton firmly and refrigerate carton on its side overnight or until firm. Alternatively, spoon chocolate mixture into a plastic wrap-lined, 1-litre-capacity container of desired shape. To remove torrone molle from carton, rip sides of carton away from torrone, using your hands or a knife.

Torrone molle will keep, refrigerated, in the carton or in an airtight container for up to 1 week. Keep refrigerated until ready to slice, and serve with coffee.
Serves 8-10

Chocolate and walnut steamed pudding with liqueur prunes

185g dark brown sugar

175g soft unsalted butter,
    plus extra, for greasing

3 eggs

100g (⅔ cup) self-raising flour

25g Dutch-process cocoa

½ teaspoon baking powder

50g (1 cup) fresh breadcrumbs

25g amaretti biscuits, crushed

50g (½ cup) chopped walnuts, roasted

Pouring cream, to serve

Liqueur prunes

1 vanilla bean, split lengthways

250g pitted prunes

110g (½ cup) caster sugar

2 tablespoons Kahlúa or Tia Maria

Using an electric mixer, beat 60g brown sugar and 50g butter until light and fluffy, then spread over base and three-quarters of the way up the side of a greased 1-litre-capacity pudding basin.

Using an electric mixer, beat remaining brown sugar and butter until light and fluffy, then add eggs, one at a time, beating well after each. Sift flour, cocoa, baking powder and a pinch of salt into a bowl, add breadcrumbs, crushed biscuits and walnuts and mix well, then fold into egg mixture until just combined. Spoon mixture into prepared basin and smooth top. Layer a piece of baking paper and foil together and fold to create a pleat in the centre, then place over top of basin and secure tightly with string. Place basin in a large saucepan, add enough boiling water to come halfway up side of basin and steam, covered, for 2 hours, checking water level every 30 minutes and replenishing, if necessary. Stand pudding for 10 minutes before turning out onto a plate.

Meanwhile, for liqueur prunes, combine scraped seeds from vanilla bean and bean, prunes, sugar, liqueur and 1 cup water in a saucepan and stir over medium heat until sugar dissolves, then simmer gently for 10 minutes. Cool to room temperature. Prunes will keep, refrigerated, in an airtight container for up to 2 weeks.

Serve sliced pudding and liqueur prunes with pouring cream. Pudding is best served on day of making.

Serves 6

19

White chocolate and nougat puddings with berries

400ml milk

400g white couverture chocolate,
    finely chopped

300g brioche crumbs or cake crumbs

100g soft butter, plus extra, for greasing

100g caster sugar

6 eggs, separated

200g soft nougat, finely chopped
    using a lightly oiled knife

Berries in sparkling shiraz carbernet

500g strawberries, hulled and quartered

400g youngberries

220g (1 cup) caster sugar

Rind of 1 lemon, cut into julienne

1 tablespoon lemon juice

160ml sparkling shiraz carbernet, chilled

For berries in sparkling shiraz cabernet, place berries in a heatproof bowl. Combine sugar, lemon rind, lemon juice and ¼ cup boiling water in a small saucepan and stir over medium heat without boiling until sugar dissolves, then pour over berries, cover and refrigerate for 1 hour or up to 8 hours.

Bring milk to the boil in a small saucepan, reduce heat, then add chocolate and whisk over low-medium heat until chocolate is melted and mixture is smooth. Remove from heat, add crumbs and stand for 10 minutes.

Using an electric mixer, beat butter and sugar until light and fluffy. Add egg yolks and butter mixture to chocolate mixture and stir until combined. Using an electric mixer, whisk egg whites until soft peaks form, then gently fold into chocolate mixture. Add nougat and mix gently. Spoon mixture into 10 greased 220ml dariole moulds or espresso cups.

Place moulds in a large baking dish or dishes, pour in enough boiling water to come halfway up sides of moulds, then cover baking dish tightly with a greased piece of foil. Bake at 160C for 40 minutes or until puddings are puffed and a cake tester withdraws clean.

Turn out puddings immediately onto 10 shallow bowls. Combine berry mixture with sparkling shiraz cabernet and spoon around puddings.

Makes 10 puddings

Note: Puddings can be served at room temperature, but they will not be as light in texture.

Chocolate and orange-liqueur mousse

250g dark couverture chocolate,
  finely chopped
100g unsalted butter, finely chopped
60ml Cointreau or other
  orange-flavoured liqueur
1 teaspoon vanilla extract
8 egg yolks, at room temperature
100g caster sugar
5 egg whites
Double cream and chocolate shavings, to serve

Combine chocolate and butter in a heatproof bowl over a saucepan of simmering water and stir until smooth and glossy. Remove from heat and whisk in liqueur and vanilla.

Using an electric mixer, whisk egg yolks and sugar until thick and pale, then gradually pour in chocolate mixture and whisk until well combined.

In another bowl, whisk egg whites with an electric mixer until stiff peaks form. Gently fold half the egg whites into chocolate mixture until just incorporated, then repeat with remaining mixture. Spoon into eight 1-cup-capacity dishes, cover and refrigerate for 6 hours or overnight until set.

Serve chocolate mousse topped with double cream and chocolate shavings. Chocolate mousse will keep, covered, in the refrigerator for up to 3 days.

Serves 8

White chocolate rice pudding

60g sultanas

2 tablespoons brandy

3 cups milk

150ml pouring cream

1 stick of cinnamon

Finely grated rind of 2 oranges

1 vanilla bean, split lengthways

200g (1 cup) arborio rice

1 tablespoon caster sugar

70g white couverture chocolate,
   finely chopped

Combine sultanas and brandy in a small bowl and stand for 30 minutes. Place milk, cream, cinnamon stick, orange rind, scraped seeds from vanilla bean and bean in a saucepan and slowly bring to just below the boil. Add rice, sugar and a pinch of salt and simmer over low heat, stirring frequently, for 30 minutes or until rice is tender and most of the liquid has been absorbed. Add sultanas, soaking liquid and chocolate, and stir until chocolate has melted. Remove cinnamon stick and vanilla bean and serve warm or cold.

Serves 4-6

Chocolate cassata

4 eggs

125g caster sugar

125g plain flour

30g cocoa

Soft butter, for greasing

Syrup

110g (½ cup) caster sugar

2 tablespoons Grand Marnier, brandy or rum

Filling

500g ricotta

80g caster sugar

80g dark chocolate, finely chopped

50g finely chopped mixed glacé fruit,
   including glacé clementine
   and glacé citron

1 teaspoon finely grated lemon rind

½ teaspoon vanilla extract

Chocolate glaze

180g dark chocolate, finely chopped

⅓ cup pouring cream

20g butter

Using an electric mixer, whisk eggs and sugar until thick and pale and mixture holds a trail. Sift together flour and cocoa, then, using a large metal spoon, gently fold into egg mixture until just combined.

Pour mixture into a greased and baking paper-lined 20cm springform tin and bake at 180C for 20-25 minutes or until firm to the touch. Stand cake in tin for 5 minutes before turning out onto a wire rack to cool completely. When cool, cut cake horizontally into 3 layers.

For syrup, combine sugar and ½ cup water in a small saucepan and bring to the boil, then simmer for 4 minutes. Remove from heat and cool to room temperature, then stir in liqueur.

For filling, using a wooden spoon, beat ricotta with sugar until smooth, then stir in remaining ingredients.

Place the bottom layer of cake, cut-side up, into a plastic wrap-lined 20cm springform cake tin. Cut middle layer into triangles and use to line the side of the tin, making sure there are no gaps. Brush base and side with half the syrup, then spoon in filling and smooth. Brush cut side of remaining cake with syrup and place cut-side down over filling, pressing down well. Brush top with remaining syrup, then cover and refrigerate for 4 hours or preferably overnight.

For chocolate glaze, combine chocolate, cream and butter in a small saucepan and stir over low heat until smooth, then cool. Invert cassata onto a large plate, cover top with chocolate glaze and refrigerate until ready to serve.

Cassata will keep, refrigerated, in an airtight container for up to 4 days.

Serves 8-10

Figs and prunes in chocolate marsala syrup

55g (¼ cup) caster sugar
125ml sweet marsala
1 vanilla bean, split lengthways
90g dark couverture chocolate, chopped
375g ready-soaked figs
170g (1 cup) pitted prunes
Double cream, to serve

Place sugar, marsala, scraped seeds from vanilla bean and
bean and ½ cup water in a saucepan and stir over low heat
until sugar dissolves. Add chocolate and cook, whisking
occasionally, over low-medium heat until chocolate is melted
and mixture is smooth. Add dried fruits and bring to a simmer,
then cook, covered, over low-medium heat for 10 minutes
or until figs and prunes are soft. Remove from heat and cool
to room temperature. Serve figs and prunes in chocolate
marsala syrup in small bowls topped with a spoonful
of double cream.
Serves 6

Self-saucing chocolate pudding

80g butter, melted, plus extra, for greasing
150g (1 cup) self-raising flour
25g (¼ cup) cocoa
75g (⅓ cup) raw caster sugar
½ cup milk
1 egg
100g (½ cup, firmly packed) brown sugar
Pouring cream, optional, to serve

Grease a 1.5-litre ovenproof dish and place on an oven tray. Sift together flour and half the cocoa, then stir in raw caster sugar. In another bowl, whisk together milk, melted butter and egg until well combined, then stir into dry ingredients until just combined. Spoon mixture into prepared dish.

Combine brown sugar and remaining cocoa, then sprinkle over top of pudding. Gradually pour 300ml boiling water, over back of a spoon, onto pudding, then cook at 170C for 40 minutes or until sponge top is cooked.

Serve immediately spooned into bowls with pouring cream, if using. Pudding is best made just before serving.

Serves 4

Chocolate panna cotta with strawberry sauce

400ml pouring cream

1 cup milk

75g (⅓ cup) caster sugar

150g dark couverture chocolate, chopped

¼ teaspoon vanilla extract

1 tablespoon powdered gelatine

Extra strawberries, optional, to serve

Strawberry sauce

250g strawberries, hulled and chopped

75g (⅓ cup) caster sugar

1 tablespoon kirsch

Combine cream, milk and sugar in a saucepan and stir over low heat until sugar dissolves and mixture is nearly boiling. Remove from heat, add chocolate and vanilla and stir until chocolate is melted and mixture is smooth.

Place 1 tablespoon hot water in a heatproof cup and sprinkle over gelatine, then stand cup in a small saucepan of simmering water and stir until gelatine dissolves. Pour gelatine mixture into cream mixture and stir until well combined, then divide among 6 lightly oiled 125ml dariole moulds. Cover and refrigerate for 2-3 hours or until set.

For strawberry sauce, process strawberries in a food processor until smooth. Transfer to a small saucepan, add sugar and stir over low heat just until sugar dissolves. Remove from heat, cool slightly, add kirsch and stir well. Cool to room temperature, then cover and refrigerate.

Dip panna cotta moulds briefly in hot water, invert panna cottas onto plates, spoon a little strawberry sauce around and serve with extra strawberries, if using.

Serves 6

Chocolate crêpes with chestnut cream

2 tablespoons Dutch-process cocoa

150g (1 cup) self-raising flour

¼ teaspoon ground cinnamon

2 teaspoons caster sugar

1 egg, lightly beaten

300ml milk

20g unsalted butter, melted,
   plus extra, for cooking

Icing sugar, for dusting

Filling

300g can unsweetened chestnut purée

1 cup double cream

¼ teaspoon vanilla extract

2 tablespoons caster sugar

1 teaspoon finely grated orange rind

For filling, combine all ingredients in a bowl and stir until smooth, then cover and refrigerate until ready to use.

Sift cocoa, flour, cinnamon and sugar into a bowl, make a well in the centre and gradually whisk in combined egg and milk until a smooth batter forms. Add melted butter and whisk until combined. Cover and stand mixture at room temperature for 30 minutes.

Melt a little extra butter in a 17cm crêpe pan over medium heat, add 2 tablespoons batter and swirl to coat base of pan with batter, then cook over medium heat until lightly browned underneath; turn and cook for another 1 minute or until lightly browned. Repeat process with extra butter and batter, stacking crêpes on top of one another as you go and keeping crêpes warm, covered, in a low oven.

Spread each crêpe with 2 tablespoons chestnut cream, fold into quarters and serve dusted liberally with icing sugar.

Makes about 12 crêpes

Serves 6

Chocolate soufflé

50g soft butter, plus extra, for greasing
2 tablespoons caster sugar
2 tablespoons plain flour
1 tablespoon cocoa
½ cup milk
75g (⅓ cup) caster sugar, extra
75g dark couverture chocolate, chopped
4 eggs, separated
Icing sugar, for dusting

Grease four 1-cup-capacity ramekins, coat with caster sugar, shaking out excess, then place ramekins on an oven tray.

Melt butter in a small saucepan until foamy, then add flour and cocoa and cook, stirring continuously, for 1 minute. Remove pan from heat and gradually whisk in milk until combined, then stir continuously over medium heat until mixture boils and thickens. Remove from heat, add extra sugar and stir until dissolved, then transfer mixture to a bowl.

Melt chocolate in a heatproof bowl over a saucepan of simmering water, then stir into milk mixture with egg yolks until well combined.

Using an electric mixer, whisk egg whites until soft peaks form. Stir one-quarter of the egg whites through chocolate mixture to lighten, then, using a large metal spoon, fold in remaining egg whites until just combined. Divide mixture among prepared ramekins and smooth tops. Cook at 190C for 18-20 minutes or until puffed. Serve immediately dusted with icing sugar.

Serves 4

Rich chocolate and muscat sorbet

1 cup freshly brewed espresso coffee
130g (⅔ cup, firmly packed) brown sugar
40g Dutch-process cocoa
60ml liqueur muscat
Ice-cream cones and grated dark chocolate, optional, to serve

Combine coffee, sugar and cocoa in a saucepan and whisk gently over medium heat until cocoa dissolves, then bring to the boil. Remove from heat and cool to room temperature. Add 2 cups water and muscat and mix well.

Freeze mixture in an ice-cream maker according to manufacturer's instructions. Alternatively, pour mixture into a freezer-proof container and stir several times during the freezing process, or transfer the nearly frozen mixture to a chilled food processor or electric mixer bowl and process or beat quickly until smooth, then return to the freezer and freeze until firm. Rich chocolate and muscat sorbet will keep, covered, in the freezer for up to 3 days.

Stand in the refrigerator for 10 minutes before serving scoops of sorbet in bowls or cones, sprinkled with grated chocolate, if using.

Serves 6-8

Ginger sablés with milk chocolate ice-cream

100g soft unsalted butter

90g icing sugar

1 egg yolk

½ teaspoon vanilla extract

140g plain flour

1 tablespoon ground ginger

Milk chocolate ice-cream

2 cups milk

2 cups pouring cream

6 egg yolks

100g caster sugar

300g milk couverture chocolate,
  coarsely chopped

Process butter and icing sugar in a food processor until well combined, then add egg yolk and vanilla and process until combined. Sift together flour and ginger, then add to butter mixture and process just until a dough forms. Form into a disc, wrap in plastic wrap and refrigerate for 40 minutes.

Roll out dough on a lightly floured surface until 5mm thick, then, using an 8cm fluted pastry cutter, cut out 16 circles and place on baking paper-lined oven trays, prick with a fork and refrigerate for 30 minutes. Bake at 190C for 12-15 minutes or until golden, then transfer to a wire rack to cool.

For milk chocolate ice-cream, bring milk and cream almost to the boil in a heavy-based saucepan. Whisk together egg yolks and sugar in a large bowl until thick and pale, gradually add milk mixture, whisking continuously until combined, then return mixture to saucepan and stir continuously over low heat until mixture thickens enough to coat the back of a spoon. Do not boil. Remove from heat and stir in milk chocolate until mixture is smooth, then cool to room temperature. Freeze mixture in an ice-cream maker according to manufacturer's instructions.

Divide half the sablés among 8 plates and top with scoops of milk chocolate ice-cream and remaining sablés and serve immediately.

Sablés will keep in an airtight container and ice-cream will keep frozen for up to 1 week.

Serves 8

Chocolate and coffee bombe

Here, the 3 ice-creams are based on 1 custard base, which is easily made. Plan to churn the ice-creams over 2 days, unless you have a refrigerator-style ice-cream maker.

2¼ cups milk
900ml pouring cream
1 teaspoon vanilla extract
9 egg yolks
220g (1 cup) caster sugar
200g dark couverture chocolate, melted
1 tablespoon instant coffee,
    dissolved in 1 tablespoon boiling water
200g white couverture chocolate, melted
Soft butter, for greasing

Combine milk, cream and vanilla in a large saucepan and bring just to the boil. Using an electric mixer, whisk egg yolks and sugar until thick and pale, then gradually stir in milk mixture until smooth. Transfer mixture to a clean saucepan, then stir continuously over low heat until mixture thickens enough to coat the back of a wooden spoon. Do not boil. Remove from heat and divide mixture evenly between 3 bowls.

Stir dark chocolate into 1 bowl of the custard mixture until smooth, then cover and refrigerate until cold. Add coffee mixture to another bowl and stir until well combined, then cover and refrigerate until cold. Stir white chocolate into remaining bowl until mixture is smooth, then cover and refrigerate until cold.

Freeze dark chocolate mixture in an ice-cream maker according to manufacturer's instructions, then spoon frozen mixture into a lightly oiled, plastic wrap-lined 10-cup-capacity pudding mould, pushing mixture up side of mould so that it is 2cm thick on base and side of mould. Cover and freeze for 1-2 hours or until firm.

Meanwhile, freeze coffee mixture in an ice-cream maker according to manufacturer's instructions, then spoon frozen mixture into mould in the same manner as for the dark chocolate. Cover and return to freezer for 1-2 hours or until firm.

Freeze white chocolate mixture in an ice-cream maker according to manufacturer's instructions, then spoon frozen mixture into mould, smooth top, cover and freeze for at least 6 hours or overnight. Remove ice-cream from freezer and immerse briefly in hot water before turning out onto a large plate. Serve bombe in slices.

Bombe will keep frozen for up to 1 week.

Serves 10-12

Bitter chocolate ice-cream sundae with caramel sauce

1 cup thickened cream

30g (¼ cup) pecans, roasted and chopped

Bitter chocolate ice-cream

2 cups milk

¼ teaspoon vanilla extract

3 egg yolks

110g (½ cup) caster sugar

150g bittersweet chocolate
   (70 per cent cocoa solids), chopped

Caramel sauce

2 tablespoons currants

2 tablespoons dark rum

220g (1 cup) caster sugar

½ cup pouring cream

40g unsalted butter, chopped

For bitter chocolate ice-cream, combine milk and vanilla in a saucepan and bring just to the boil. Using an electric mixer, whisk egg yolks and sugar until thick and pale, then gradually stir in milk until combined. Return mixture to pan and stir continuously over low heat until mixture thickens enough to coat the back of a wooden spoon. Do not boil. Remove from heat and stir in chocolate until smooth, cool to room temperature, then cover and refrigerate until cold. Freeze chocolate mixture in an ice-cream maker according to manufacturer's instructions.

For caramel sauce, combine currants and rum in a small bowl and stand for 10 minutes. Combine sugar with ⅓ cup water in a small saucepan and stir over low heat until sugar dissolves. Increase heat and boil, without stirring, until syrup is a caramel colour. Remove from heat, cool slightly, then stir in cream and butter, taking care as mixture will spit. Stir in currant mixture, then cool to room temperature. Makes about 1 cup caramel sauce.

To serve, whip cream until soft peaks form. Place scoops of ice-cream in parfait glasses, top with a little whipped cream, then repeat layers until glasses are full. Pour caramel sauce over and sprinkle with pecans. Serve immediately.

Bitter chocolate ice-cream will keep frozen, and caramel sauce will keep refrigerated, for up to 1 week.

Serves 4

Frozen espresso mousse with chocolate sauce

110g (½ cup) caster sugar

½ cup freshly brewed espresso coffee

4 egg yolks

2 tablespoons finely ground espresso coffee

2 tablespoons Kahlúa or Tia Maria

1 cup pouring cream,
   whipped until soft peaks form

Chocolate sauce

110g (½ cup) caster sugar

50g dark chocolate, chopped

100ml Kahlúa or Tia Maria

For chocolate sauce, combine sugar with ¼ cup water in a small saucepan and, without stirring, slowly bring to a simmer. Increase heat and boil for 5 minutes or until deep golden, then quickly remove from heat and add ½ cup water, taking care as mixture will spit. Return mixture to low heat and stir for 5 minutes or until smooth. Cool slightly, then stir in chocolate and liqueur, stirring until chocolate melts and mixture is smooth. Cool. Thin sauce with a little boiling water if it thickens too much on standing. Store chocolate sauce in the refrigerator and bring to room temperature before serving. Makes about 1½ cups chocolate sauce.

Combine sugar and coffee in a small saucepan, stir over medium heat for 5 minutes or until sugar dissolves, then boil for 3 minutes and remove from heat. Cool slightly. Using an electric mixer, whisk egg yolks until pale and thick and mixture holds a trail. With motor running, slowly pour hot coffee syrup onto yolks in a thin stream, then whisk at high speed until mixture is very thick and holds a trail. Continue whisking until mixture is cool, then stir in ground coffee and liqueur until just combined. Gently fold in cream, then divide mixture among 4 chilled 200ml glasses and freeze for 8 hours or overnight. Serve frozen mousse with chocolate sauce passed separately.

Mousse can be made up to 2 days ahead.

Serves 4

White chocolate and coconut tartufi

4 egg yolks

150g caster sugar

1 teaspoon cornflour

600ml pouring cream

300ml milk

60ml Malibu

160g white couverture chocolate, chopped

30g shredded coconut, toasted until golden

50g drained amarena cherries

250g dark chocolate, chopped

Toasted shaved coconut, optional, to serve

Using an electric mixer, whisk egg yolks, sugar and cornflour until thick and pale.

Combine cream and milk in a large saucepan and bring nearly to the boil. Gradually whisk cream mixture into egg yolk mixture until well combined. Return mixture to saucepan, add 2 tablespoons liqueur and stir continuously over low heat until mixture thickens enough to coat the back of a wooden spoon. Do not boil. Transfer custard to a large bowl, add white chocolate and stir until smooth, then cool. Stir shredded coconut into custard and freeze mixture in an ice-cream maker according to manufacturer's instructions, then transfer to a container and freeze until firm.

Combine cherries and remaining liqueur in a small bowl and set aside for 15 minutes.

Line a metal tray with foil and place in freezer for 10 minutes. Using a small ice-cream scoop or large melon-baller, scoop balls of ice-cream and place on foil-lined tray. Using a small spoon, scoop out the centre of each ice-cream ball and fill each with a liqueur cherry, then cover over hole with a little of the scooped-out ice-cream. Freeze until firm.

Melt dark chocolate in a heatproof bowl over a saucepan of simmering water, then pour into a small, deep bowl or cup. Remove ice-cream balls from freezer, insert a toothpick into each and dip into chocolate, then return to tray. Coat half the balls in shaved coconut, if using, then freeze until ready to serve. Tartufi will keep frozen for up to 3 days.

Makes about 18

Chocolate Catalan cake

175g soft unsalted butter,
  plus extra, for greasing
175g dark brown sugar
3 eggs
200g (1⅓ cups) self-raising flour
20g Dutch-process cocoa
125g finely chopped glacé clementine
  or glacé orange
120g dark couverture chocolate,
  coarsely chopped
80ml sweet marsala
100g (⅔ cup) pinenuts

Using an electric mixer, beat butter and sugar until light and fluffy, then add eggs, one at a time, beating well after each. Sift flour, cocoa and a pinch of salt into a large bowl, then stir in glacé clementine. Stir flour mixture and chopped chocolate into egg mixture, alternately with marsala, until mixture is just combined. Spoon mixture into a greased and base-lined 20cm round cake tin, smooth top, then sprinkle with pinenuts. Bake at 180C for 55-65 minutes or until a cake tester withdraws with moist crumbs attached, covering with a loose piece of foil halfway through cooking. Stand cake in tin for 10 minutes before turning out onto a wire rack to cool. Cake will keep in an airtight container for up to 1 week.
Serves 8-10

Pampepato

Pampepato is a chocolate-coated spice cake that is traditionally made at Christmas in the Emilia-Romagna region of Italy. The pepper flavour becomes stronger the longer the cake is stored.

450g (3 cups) plain flour, plus extra, for dusting
½ teaspoon baking powder
½ teaspoon bicarbonate of soda
75g glacé citron, chopped into 1cm pieces
Grated rind of 2 oranges
6 small dried figs, stems removed, thinly sliced
100g whole blanched almonds,
   roasted and coarsely chopped
330g (1½ cups) caster sugar
125g (1¼ cups) cocoa
1 teaspoon freshly ground black pepper
¼ teaspoon ground cardamom
¼ teaspoon ground cloves
Soft butter, for greasing
200g bittersweet chocolate
   (70 per cent cocoa solids), chopped

Sift flour, baking powder and bicarbonate of soda into a large bowl, then add glacé citron, orange rind, figs and almonds and mix well.

Place sugar, cocoa, spices and 1¼ cups water in a small saucepan and whisk over medium heat until combined. Do not boil. Pour cocoa mixture over dry ingredients and mix to form a firm, slightly sticky dough. Divide mixture in half and, using your hands, form each half into a 7cm round cake, about 2cm thick.

Place cakes on greased and floured oven trays and bake at 150C for 1 hour or until a cake tester withdraws clean. Cool cakes on trays, then cover with plastic wrap and leave, at room temperature, for at least 12 hours for flavours to develop.

Melt chocolate in a heatproof bowl over a saucepan of simmering water.

Place cakes upside-down on a wire rack, spread each with a thin layer of melted chocolate and leave to set, then turn cakes over and spread tops with a thin layer of melted chocolate. When chocolate is set, serve pampepato cut into long, thin slices.

Unglazed pampepato will keep, covered in plastic wrap, in a cool, dry, dark place for up to 1 month.

Makes 2 cakes

White chocolate mousse cake

150g butter, chopped
150g dark chocolate, chopped
220g (1 cup) caster sugar
200ml milk
150g (1 cup) self-raising flour
75g (½ cup) plain flour
¼ cup cocoa
2 eggs
Icing sugar, optional, for dusting

White chocolate mousse

150g white couverture
   chocolate, chopped
60g unsalted butter, chopped
1 egg, separated
200ml thickened cream

For white chocolate mousse, melt chocolate and butter in a heatproof bowl over a saucepan of simmering water. Remove from heat, cool slightly, then whisk in egg yolk; mixture will separate, so continue whisking until smooth. Whip cream until firm peaks form and fold into chocolate mixture. Whisk egg white until firm peaks form and gently fold into chocolate mixture. Cover and refrigerate until just firm.

Combine butter, chocolate, sugar and milk in a saucepan and stir over low heat until chocolate melts and sugar dissolves, then remove from heat. Sift flours and cocoa into mixture and mix well. Add eggs one at a time, mixing well after each, and stir until smooth. Pour into a greased and base-lined 22cm round cake tin and bake at 160C for 75 minutes, or until a cake tester withdraws clean. Stand in tin for 10 minutes before turning out onto a wire rack to cool.

Split cake horizontally, place bottom half in a base-lined 22cm springform pan and spread with white chocolate mousse, replace top and refrigerate for 2 hours or until firm. Cake will keep, refrigerated, in an airtight container for up to 2 days. Remove from refrigerator 30 minutes before serving and dust with icing sugar, if using.

Serves 8-10

Gianduja marjolaine

Marjolaine is the name given to this classic hazelnut meringue layered cake created by the late French chef, Fernand Point. This recipe is a simplified version of his classic, using just one filling, gianduja (hazelnut and chocolate paste), instead of Point's three.

220g (1 cup) caster sugar
185g (1¼ cups) roasted peeled hazelnuts, chopped
1 tablespoon cornflour
6 egg whites
Gianduja filling
100g (⅔ cup) roasted peeled hazelnuts
50g icing sugar
100g dark couverture chocolate, melted
1 cup pouring cream, whisked until soft peaks form
Ganache
250g dark couverture chocolate, chopped
½ cup pouring cream

Combine 55g (¼ cup) of the caster sugar, hazelnuts and cornflour in a food processor and process until finely ground. Using an electric mixer, whisk egg whites until foamy, add a pinch of salt and whisk until soft peaks form, then gradually add remaining sugar and whisk until mixture is thick and glossy. Carefully fold nut mixture into egg white mixture in 2 batches until just combined. Spoon mixture into a baking paper-lined 1.5cm-deep 26x32cm oven tray, smooth top and bake at 180C for 25 minutes or until golden. Stand meringue in tray for 10 minutes, then turn out onto a wire rack covered with a piece of baking paper and carefully peel off baking paper lining. Cool.

For gianduja filling, process hazelnuts and icing sugar in a food processor until a smooth, oily paste forms (this will take about 5 minutes and you will need to keep scraping down the side of the bowl). Add melted chocolate and process until combined and mixture is smooth. Transfer gianduja to a bowl, stir in one-third of the whipped cream to loosen, then fold in remaining whipped cream until just combined.

For ganache, process chopped chocolate in a food processor until the size of large breadcrumbs. Bring cream just to the boil in a small saucepan. With food processor running, add hot cream to chocolate and process until mixture is smooth. Transfer to a small bowl and cool at room temperature until thick and of spreading consistency.

Cut hazelnut meringue into 4 widthways. Place a meringue rectangle on a serving plate and spread with one-third gianduja filling, then repeat layering twice more, finishing with a layer of meringue. Spread top and sides of cake with ganache and refrigerate until set.

Cake will keep, refrigerated, in an airtight container for up to 1 week.

Serves 8-10

Chocolate-orange poppy seed cakes

110g (¾ cup) self-raising flour

2 tablespoons Dutch-process cocoa

¾ teaspoon baking powder

60g soft unsalted butter

75g (⅓ cup) caster sugar

2 eggs

1½ tablespoons milk

2 tablespoons poppy seeds

Orange icing

90g cream cheese, softened

1 egg

55g (¼ cup) caster sugar

1 tablespoon finely chopped glacé orange

Sift flour, cocoa and baking powder into a bowl.

Using an electric mixer, beat butter and sugar until light and fluffy. Add eggs, one at a time, beating well after each. Fold flour mixture into butter mixture alternately with milk, then stir in poppy seeds until well combined.

Line a 6-hole (⅓-cup-capacity) muffin tin with paper cases, then divide mixture among cases and bake at 180C for 25 minutes or until a cake tester withdraws clean. Cool cakes in tin for 5 minutes before turning out onto a wire rack to cool.

For orange icing, using a wooden spoon, combine cream cheese, egg and sugar in a small bowl and beat until smooth. Spread 1 tablespoon icing over the top of each cake, then sprinkle with glacé orange.

Cakes will keep in an airtight container for 2-3 days.

Makes 6

Brazo de gitano

This Spanish cake translates as 'gypsy's arm' as it is said to resemble the tanned arm of a gypsy.

200g dark couverture chocolate, chopped
6 eggs, separated
110g (½ cup) caster sugar
Soft butter, for greasing
Cocoa, for dusting
Filling
1½ cups thickened cream
140g dark couverture chocolate, coarsely chopped
2 teaspoons brandy
2 teaspoons sambuca or ouzo

Combine chocolate with ¼ cup water in a small saucepan and stir over medium heat until smooth. Cool.

Using an electric mixer, whisk egg yolks and sugar until thick and pale, then stir in chocolate mixture and set aside.

Using an electric mixer, whisk egg whites and ¼ teaspoon salt until soft peaks form, then fold into chocolate mixture, in three batches, until just combined. Spoon mixture into a greased and baking paper-lined 24x30cm swiss roll pan and smooth surface, then bake at 180C for 18-20 minutes or until the cake springs back when lightly pressed. Turn out cake onto a piece of baking paper dusted with cocoa. Working while cake is hot, gently roll up cake from long side, using the paper as a guide.

For filling, combine ½ cup cream and chocolate in a small saucepan and stir over low-medium heat until smooth, then stir in brandy and liqueur, remove from heat and cool. Using an electric mixer, whisk remaining cream until soft peaks form, then fold into cooled chocolate mixture. Refrigerate chocolate mixture for 30 minutes or until firm. Gently unroll the cake and spread evenly with filling, leaving a 2cm border. Re-roll cake (cake may crack a little), then cover with plastic wrap and refrigerate for 30 minutes or until filling is firm. Serve dusted with cocoa. Cake will keep, refrigerated, in an airtight container for up to 3 days.

Serves 8

Chocolate-raisin cake with tokay mascarpone

This cake will cut better if made a day ahead.

75g raisins

1½ tablespoons tokay

350g dark couverture chocolate, chopped

150g unsalted butter, chopped,
    plus extra, for greasing

110g (½ cup) caster sugar

¼ cup freshly brewed espresso coffee

50g (⅓ cup) self-raising flour

35g (⅓ cup) Dutch-process cocoa

4 eggs, separated

75g (⅓ cup) caster sugar, extra

Tokay mascarpone

50ml tokay

350g mascarpone

1 tablespoon icing sugar

Soak raisins in tokay for 1 hour. Melt chocolate, butter, sugar and coffee in a heatproof bowl over a saucepan of simmering water, stirring occasionally, until smooth and glossy. Remove from heat and stand for 5 minutes.

Stir combined sifted flour and cocoa into chocolate mixture and mix until combined. Add egg yolks, raisins and tokay and mix well.

Using an electric mixer, whisk egg whites until soft peaks form, then add extra sugar and continue whisking until stiff peaks form. Fold egg white mixture into chocolate mixture, one-third at a time. Spoon mixture into a greased and baking paper-lined 23cm springform pan and bake at 180C for 60 minutes or until edge is cooked and a cake tester inserted in the centre withdraws with moist crumbs attached. Cool completely in pan.

For tokay mascarpone, whisk together all ingredients until well combined and serve with cake, passed separately. Cake will keep in an airtight container for up to 3 days.

Serves 8-10

Chocolate, almond and white chocolate brownies

125g soft unsalted butter, plus extra, for greasing

110g (½ cup) caster sugar

2 eggs

40g (⅓ cup) ground almonds

65g plain flour

½ teaspoon baking powder

2 tablespoons Dutch-process cocoa

125g dark couverture chocolate, melted

100g white couverture chocolate, chopped

Using an electric mixer, beat butter and sugar until light and fluffy. Add eggs, one at a time, beating well after each. Stir in ground almonds, sifted flour, baking powder and cocoa and mix until well combined. Stir in melted chocolate and white chocolate, then spoon into a greased and base-lined 20cm square cake tin and bake at 170C for 40 minutes or until a cake tester withdraws clean.

Stand in tin for 5 minutes before turning out onto a wire rack to cool. Serve cut into 3cm squares. Brownies will keep for up to 4 days in an airtight container.

Makes about 40 pieces

Chocolate and orange marble cake

80g dark chocolate, chopped
150g soft unsalted butter,
   plus extra, for greasing
200g caster sugar
1 teaspoon vanilla extract
2 eggs
300g (2 cups) self-raising flour, sifted
½ cup milk
2 tablespoons orange juice
Finely grated rind of 1 orange
Glaze
100g dark chocolate, chopped
50g unsalted butter, chopped

Melt chocolate in a heatproof bowl over a saucepan of simmering water. Remove pan from heat and stand chocolate in bowl over water.

Meanwhile, using an electric mixer, beat butter, sugar and vanilla until light and fluffy. Add eggs one at a time, beating well after each, then gently stir in flour and milk alternately. Divide mixture in half, add orange juice and rind to one half and melted chocolate to the other, then stir each mixture until well combined.

Drop large spoonfuls of each mixture alternately into a greased and base-lined 7cm-deep 7x26cm rectangular tin, then, using a flat bladed knife, cut through mixture using a swirling motion to give a marbled effect. Bake at 180C for 1 hour or until a cake tester withdraws clean. Stand cake in tin for 5 minutes before turning out onto a wire rack over a tray to cool completely.

For glaze, place chocolate and butter in a heatproof bowl over a saucepan of simmering water, stir occasionally until melted and smooth, then pour immediately over cooled cake. Stand cake at room temperature until glaze is set, then serve cut into slices.

Cake will keep, refrigerated, in an airtight container for up to 3 days.
Serves 8-10

Queen of Sheba cake

250g dark couverture
  chocolate, chopped
150g ($\frac{2}{3}$ cup) caster sugar
150g unsalted butter, chopped,
  plus extra, for greasing
1 tablespoon brandy
1 tablespoon freshly brewed
  espresso coffee
125g ground almonds or hazelnuts
5 eggs, separated
Chocolate topping
200g dark couverture
  chocolate, chopped
60g unsalted butter, chopped

Combine chocolate, sugar, butter, brandy and coffee in a heatproof bowl over a saucepan of simmering water. Stir occasionally until chocolate is melted and mixture is smooth, then transfer to a large bowl and stir in ground almonds. Whisk in egg yolks, one at a time, until well combined.

Using an electric mixer, whisk egg whites until firm peaks form, then fold a large spoonful of egg whites into chocolate mixture to lighten. Using a large metal spoon, fold in remaining egg whites until just incorporated. Spoon mixture into a greased and base-lined 20cm square cake tin, then bake at 180C for 45-50 minutes or until cake is firm to the touch, but still a little soft in the centre. Cool cake in pan; the cake will sink a little as it cools. Carefully remove cake from pan and place on a wire rack over a tray to cool.

For chocolate topping, combine chocolate and butter in a heatproof bowl over a saucepan of simmering water and stir occasionally until smooth. Cool for 15-20 minutes or until thickened, then pour over top of cake. Using a palette knife, smooth topping over top of cake and stand at room temperature until set.

Cake will keep, refrigerated, in an airtight container for up to 3 days.

Serves 10

Chocolate and hazelnut cake with marmalade ice-cream

225g bittersweet chocolate (70 per cent
   cocoa solids), refrigerated until cold,
   then finely grated

200g ground hazelnuts

8 eggs, separated

250g caster sugar

Finely grated rind of 1 large orange

2 teaspoons vanilla extract

100g unsalted butter, melted and cooled,
   plus extra, for greasing

Cocoa, for dusting

Marmalade ice-cream

1½ cups pouring cream

1½ cups milk

50g caster sugar

170g (½ cup) sweet orange marmalade

8 egg yolks

For marmalade ice-cream, combine cream and milk in a heavy-based saucepan and bring just to the boil. Whisk sugar, marmalade and egg yolks until well combined, then slowly whisk in cream mixture. Return mixture to pan and stir continuously over low heat until it thickens enough to coat the back of a wooden spoon. Do not boil. Cool to room temperature, then freeze mixture in an ice-cream maker according to manufacturer's instructions.

Combine grated chocolate and ground hazelnuts in a large bowl.

Using an electric mixer, whisk egg yolks and sugar until thick and pale, add orange rind and vanilla and whisk until just combined, then set aside.

Using an electric mixer, whisk egg whites and ¼ teaspoon salt until stiff peaks form.

Add egg yolk mixture, one-third of the whisked egg whites, and melted butter to grated chocolate mixture and stir until well combined, then gently fold in remaining egg whites until just incorporated.

Spoon mixture into a greased and floured 24cm springform pan, level top and bake at 180C for 20 minutes, then cover with baking paper and bake for another 25 minutes or until a cake tester withdraws clean. Stand cake in pan for 15 minutes before transferring to a wire rack to cool.

Dust cooled cake with cocoa and serve slices with scoops of marmalade ice-cream. Cake will keep in an airtight container and ice-cream will keep frozen for up to 5 days.

Serves 8-10

Chocolate macaroons

3 egg whites
200g caster sugar
1½ tablespoons plain flour
25g (¼ cup) cocoa
150g ground almonds

Using an electric mixer, whisk egg whites until soft
peaks form, then gradually add sugar, whisking well
after each addition to dissolve sugar, until mixture is
smooth and glossy.

Sift flour and cocoa together, then stir in ground
almonds. Gently stir flour mixture into egg white
mixture until just combined. Spoon tablespoonfuls of
mixture onto a baking paper-lined oven tray and bake at
180C for 10-15 minutes or until crisp on the outside but
still soft in the centre. Stand macaroons for 10 minutes,
then transfer to a wire rack to cool. Macaroons will keep
in an airtight container for up to 1 week.

Makes about 24

Baci di dama

Ingredients can be halved to make fewer biscuits.

250g soft unsalted butter
110g (²⁄₃ cup) icing sugar, sifted
1½ teaspoons vanilla extract
250g (1²⁄₃ cups) plain flour
50g (½ cup) cocoa
105g (¾ cup) hazelnuts, roasted,
 peeled and finely ground
Filling
125g dark chocolate, chopped
30g unsalted butter
75g (½ cup) hazelnuts, roasted,
 peeled and finely ground

Using an electric mixer, beat butter and icing sugar until light and fluffy, then add vanilla. Sift together flour and cocoa and stir into butter mixture with ground hazelnuts until mixture is well combined. Take heaped tablespoons of mixture and, using your hands, roll into balls, then place on baking paper-lined oven trays and flatten slightly with your fingers. Refrigerate biscuits for 2 hours or overnight, then bake at 180C for 15 minutes or until firm to the touch. Cool on trays for 5 minutes, then carefully transfer to wire racks to cool completely.

For filling, melt chocolate and butter in a small heatproof bowl over a saucepan of simmering water, then remove from heat, add ground hazelnuts and stir to combine well. Spread a little filling onto half of the cooled biscuits, then top with remaining biscuits. Leave in a cool place for filling to set.

Filled biscuits will keep in an airtight container for up to 1 week, or in the freezer for up to 3 months.
Makes about 60

Bitter chocolate and espresso sandwiches

200g (1⅓ cups) plain flour
75g (¾ cup) Dutch-process cocoa
175g soft unsalted butter
220g (1 cup) caster sugar
Espresso filling
60g soft unsalted butter
500g icing sugar, sifted
¼ cup freshly brewed espresso coffee

Sift flour, cocoa and ½ teaspoon salt into a bowl. Using an electric mixer, beat butter and sugar until light and fluffy, then gradually add flour mixture and beat until just combined. Turn out mixture onto a lightly floured surface and knead until just smooth, then divide in half.

Roll out each half of dough between sheets of baking paper until 2-3mm thick, then, using a floured 5.5cm pastry cutter, cut rounds from dough and place on baking paper-lined oven trays. Repeat process, re-rolling dough scraps. Gently press tines of a fork around outer edge of half of the rounds, prick centres several times, then bake rounds, in batches, at 190C for 8-10 minutes or until firm to the touch. Stand biscuits on trays for 5 minutes before transferring to wire racks to cool. Unfilled biscuits will keep in an airtight container for up to 5 days.

Meanwhile, for espresso filling, combine all ingredients in a heatproof bowl over a saucepan of simmering water and stir until smooth. Remove bowl from heat and refrigerate for 20 minutes, stirring every 5 minutes, or until very thick and creamy.

Spread undecorated biscuits with a little espresso filling and sandwich together with decorated tops. Filled biscuits will keep in an airtight container for up to 3 days.
Makes about 32 filled biscuits

Chocolate shortbread spirals

160g soft unsalted butter
80g caster sugar
150g (1 cup) plain flour, sifted
80g ground rice

Chocolate shortbread

165g soft unsalted butter
100g caster sugar
150g (1 cup) plain flour, sifted
60g ground rice
40g Dutch-process cocoa, sifted

Using an electric mixer, beat butter and sugar until light and fluffy. Add flour and ground rice to butter mixture and stir until mixture forms a dough. Place dough between 2 sheets of baking paper and roll out to form a 25x30cm rectangle, then set aside.

For chocolate shortbread, using an electric mixer, beat butter and sugar until light and fluffy. Add flour, ground rice and cocoa to butter mixture and stir until mixture forms a dough. Place dough between 2 sheets of baking paper and roll out to form a 25x30cm rectangle.

Carefully place plain dough on top of chocolate dough and trim edges. Using baking paper as a guide, roll up firmly to form a log (dough may crack on first turns). Place rolled dough, wrapped in baking paper, on an oven tray and refrigerate for 1 hour or until firm. Trim ends and cut into 1cm-thick slices. Place 5cm apart on baking paper-lined oven trays and bake at 170C for 40 minutes, swapping trays from top to bottom after 20 minutes, or until pale golden and firm.

Stand biscuits on trays for 5 minutes before transferring to wire racks to cool.

Biscuits will keep in an airtight container for up to 4 days.

Makes about 30

Chocolate cherry biscotti

270g (¾ cup) amarena cherries in syrup
300g (2 cups) plain flour
50g (½ cup) cocoa, plus extra, for dusting
1 teaspoon baking powder
220g (1 cup) caster sugar
3 eggs
1 teaspoon vanilla extract

Strain cherries, reserving syrup. Sift together flour, cocoa and baking powder, then add sugar and strained cherries and stir to combine. In another bowl, whisk together eggs, vanilla and 1 tablespoon of reserved cherry syrup, then stir into dry ingredients until mixture forms a dough. Divide dough in half and roll out each piece on a work surface dusted lightly with extra cocoa, to form a 25cm log. Place each log on a baking paper-lined oven tray and bake at 180C for 25-30 minutes or until firm to the touch. Stand on trays until completely cooled.

Using a serrated knife, cut logs on the diagonal into 1cm-thick slices, then place on baking paper-lined oven trays and bake at 140C for another 25-30 minutes or until dry, then transfer to wire racks to cool.

Biscotti will keep in an airtight container for up to 3 days.
Makes about 28

Spiced honey and chocolate biscuits

250g (1⅔ cups) plain flour
Pinch of freshly grated nutmeg
Pinch of ground cardamom
½ teaspoon ground ginger
¼ teaspoon ground cinnamon
1 teaspoon baking powder
75g (⅓ cup) caster sugar
50g honey
1 tablespoon milk
80g butter, chopped
1 egg, lightly beaten
200g dark couverture
   chocolate, melted

Sift flour, spices and baking powder into a large bowl, then stir in sugar. Combine honey, milk and butter in a small saucepan and stir over low heat until butter is just melted and mixture well combined. Cool slightly.

Add honey mixture and beaten egg to flour mixture and, using a wooden spoon, mix to form a soft dough. Form heaped teaspoonfuls of mixture into balls, then roll into 11cm-long sticks, place on baking paper-lined oven trays and bake at 170C for 15 minutes. Stand biscuits on trays for 5 minutes before transferring to wire racks to cool slightly.

Spoon melted chocolate into a narrow, deep container so that when biscuits are dipped, the chocolate will reach one-third of the way up biscuits. When biscuits are cool enough to handle but still slightly warm, dip biscuits, one at a time, into chocolate, shake away excess, then place on baking paper-lined trays and stand until chocolate is set. Biscuits will keep in an airtight container, stored in a cool place, for up to 3 days.

Makes about 44

Chocolate marzipan slice

185g (1¼ cups) plain flour

25g (¼ cup) cocoa

85g caster sugar

115g cold unsalted butter, chopped

1 egg, lightly beaten

1 egg, extra, lightly beaten, for glazing

Filling

400g marzipan

30g dark chocolate chips or buttons,
  coarsely chopped

30g blanched almonds, coarsely chopped

1 teaspoon finely grated lemon rind

1 tablespoon brandy

Sift flour, cocoa, sugar and a pinch of salt into a bowl, then add butter and, using fingertips, rub in until mixture resembles coarse breadcrumbs. Make a well in the centre, add beaten egg, then, using a flat-bladed knife, mix until mixture almost comes together. Form dough into a ball, flatten slightly, then wrap in plastic wrap and refrigerate for 2 hours.

Meanwhile, for filling, crumble marzipan into a bowl, then add remaining ingredients and stir until well combined. Roll marzipan mixture into a sausage shape 2.5-3cm in diameter and 36cm long, then refrigerate until needed.

Roll out pastry between 2 sheets of baking paper to form a 13x28cm rectangle, then refrigerate on baking paper for 30 minutes.

Brush pastry with extra beaten egg, then place marzipan log lengthways down centre of dough and roll dough around marzipan to form a tight cylinder. Place roll, seam-side down, on a baking paper-lined oven tray and brush with extra beaten egg, then refrigerate for 10 minutes or until egg is dry. Bake at 180C for 25 minutes or until pastry is firm to the touch. Cool on oven tray. Cut cooled roll on the diagonal into 1cm-thick slices.

Chocolate marzipan slice will keep in an airtight container for up to 3 days.

Makes about 20

Chocolate pithiviers

50g dark couverture chocolate, chopped

120g caster sugar

2 tablespoons Dutch-process cocoa

150g ground almonds

100g cold unsalted butter, finely chopped

3 eggs

2 teaspoons brandy

6 sheets of frozen butter puff pastry, thawed

Process chocolate, sugar, cocoa and ground almonds in a food processor until chocolate is very finely chopped. Add butter and process until mixture begins to come together. Add 2 eggs and brandy and process until well combined. Transfer mixture to a bowl, cover and refrigerate for 2 hours or until mixture is firm.

Cut sixteen 12cm circles from puff pastry and place 8 on baking paper-lined oven trays. Beat remaining egg lightly and brush edges of pastry rounds on trays with egg, then divide filling among rounds, mounding it in the middle and leaving a 2cm border. Place remaining pastry rounds over filling, pressing edges together to join, then, using the back of a knife, make indents at 1.5cm intervals around pastry edge to create a scalloped edge. Brush with egg mixture, then refrigerate for 15 minutes or until glaze is dry. Using a small sharp knife, make a pinwheel pattern on top of each pithivier, making sure the knife does not cut all the way through pastry and stopping short of the scalloped edge, then make a small cut in top of pastry to allow the steam to escape.

Bake at 200C for 10 minutes, then reduce oven temperature to 180C and bake for another 15-20 minutes or until golden and risen. Stand for 10 minutes before serving warm or at room temperature.

Pithiviers are best served on day of making.

Makes 8

Chocolate, walnut and honey tart

225g (1½ cups) plain flour, sifted

2 tablespoons icing sugar

150g cold unsalted butter, chopped

1 egg yolk

Icing sugar, for dusting

Whipped cream, optional, to serve

Filling

150g dark couverture chocolate, chopped

150g unsalted butter, chopped

55g (¼ cup) caster sugar

3 eggs

¼ teaspoon vanilla extract

¼ cup honey

120g walnuts, roasted and finely chopped

Process flour, icing sugar and butter in a food processor until mixture resembles coarse breadcrumbs. Add egg yolk and 2 tablespoons iced water and process until mixture just comes together. Form into a disc, wrap in plastic wrap and refrigerate for 1 hour.

Roll out pastry on a lightly floured surface until 5mm thick and line a 24cm tart tin with removable base, then refrigerate for 30 minutes. Line tart shell with baking paper, fill with dried beans or rice and bake at 180C for 15 minutes, then remove paper and beans and bake for another 5-8 minutes or until pastry is golden and dry. Cool.

For filling, place chocolate and butter in a heatproof bowl over a saucepan of simmering water and stir occasionally until smooth. Remove from heat and cool.

In a separate bowl, place sugar, eggs, vanilla and a pinch of salt and whisk until well combined. Add honey and stir until combined, then fold in chocolate mixture until well combined. Sprinkle walnuts over base of pastry, then pour chocolate filling over. Bake tart at 180C for 25 minutes or until filling is set and a cake tester withdraws clean. Transfer tart to a wire rack and cool to room temperature. Dust chocolate tart with icing sugar and serve with whipped cream, if using. Tart will keep in an airtight container for up to 2 days.

Serves 6

White chocolate and geranium-water tarts

275g plain flour
150g cold unsalted butter, finely chopped,
    plus extra, for greasing
50g icing sugar, sifted
1 egg
35g (¼ cup) slivered or chopped pistachios
120g raspberries
Icing sugar, optional, for dusting
Filling
½ cup pouring cream
½ teaspoon geranium water or rose water
125g white couverture chocolate, finely chopped
1 egg, at room temperature, separated

Process flour, butter, icing sugar and a pinch of salt in a food processor until mixture resembles breadcrumbs, then add egg and process until mixture just comes together. Divide mixture in half, form each half into a disc, then wrap both halves in plastic wrap and refrigerate for 2 hours.

Roll out one-half of the pastry until 2-3mm thick and, using a 7cm pastry cutter, cut out 12 rounds and place in greased 6cm tart tins, then prick bases. Repeat the process with remaining pastry. Line pastry with baking paper, fill with dried beans or rice and bake at 200C for 7 minutes, then remove paper and beans and bake for another 5-7 minutes or until dry and light golden. Cool.

Meanwhile, for filling, bring cream just to the boil in a small saucepan, add geranium water, then pour over white chocolate in a bowl and stir until smooth. Cool white chocolate mixture to room temperature, then whisk in egg yolk until well combined. Using a metal whisk, whisk egg white until stiff peaks form, then gently fold into white chocolate mixture until just combined.

Spoon 1 tablespoon of filling into each tart shell and bake at 190C for 10-12 minutes or until filling is just set and golden. Carefully lift tarts from tins and place on a wire rack, then scatter half with pistachios and half with raspberries. Dust with icing sugar, if using. Serve tarts warm or at room temperature. Undecorated tarts will keep, refrigerated, in an airtight container for up to 3 days.
Makes 24

Chocolate babka

1 cup lukewarm milk

110g (½ cup) caster sugar

7g dried yeast

600g (4 cups) plain flour

2 egg yolks, lightly beaten

120g soft unsalted butter

1 teaspoon finely grated
   lemon rind

Icing sugar, for dusting

Filling

55g (¼ cup) caster sugar

35g (¼ cup) plain flour

40g unsalted butter, chopped

100g dark chocolate, chopped

60g pecans, chopped

Place milk in a small bowl, stir in 1 teaspoon sugar, sprinkle over yeast and stand for 10 minutes or until mixture is foamy. Sift remaining sugar, flour and ½ teaspoon salt into a large bowl, make a well in the centre and pour in the yeast mixture, then add egg yolks, butter and lemon rind. Using a wooden spoon, beat mixture until a soft, but not sticky, dough forms, adding a little extra milk if necessary. Turn out onto a lightly floured surface and knead for 10 minutes or until smooth and elastic. Form dough into a ball, place in a greased bowl, turn to coat, then cover with plastic wrap and leave in a draught-free place for 1½-2 hours or until doubled in size.

Meanwhile, for filling, combine sugar and flour in a bowl, add butter and, using fingertips, rub in butter until mixture resembles breadcrumbs, then stir in chocolate and pecans.

Knock down dough, then turn out onto a lightly floured surface and knead gently for 2 minutes. Using a rolling pin, roll out dough to form a 25x40cm rectangle, then sprinkle filling over dough, leaving a 2cm border. Roll up tightly from long side, pinching edges to seal. Carefully lift the rolled dough and ease it into a lightly greased 25cm kugelhopf tin. Cover with plastic wrap and leave in a draught-free place for 1 hour or until doubled in size. Alternatively, place dough in the refrigerator and leave to rise slowly overnight.

Bake babka at 190C for 10 minutes, reduce oven temperature to 180C and bake for another 20-25 minutes or until golden. Remove from tin and turn out onto an oven tray. Return to oven and bake for another 5 minutes or until babka sounds hollow when tapped. Serve babka warm or at room temperature dusted with icing sugar and cut into slices.

Babka will keep in an airtight container for up to 2 days.

Serves 8

Pain au chocolat

360ml lukewarm milk
55g (¼ cup) caster sugar, plus extra, for sprinkling
8g dried yeast
450g (3 cups) plain flour, approximately
60g butter, chopped
2 x 100g bars Lindt Excellence dark chocolate
1 egg white and 1 tablespoon caster sugar,
  lightly whisked
Bowls of milky hot chocolate, optional, to serve

Place ¼ cup (60ml) lukewarm milk in a small bowl, stir in 1 teaspoon sugar, sprinkle over yeast and stand for 10 minutes or until mixture is foamy.

Sift flour into a large bowl and, using fingertips, rub in butter until mixture resembles fine breadcrumbs, then stir in remaining milk, yeast mixture and remaining sugar and stir to form a soft dough (add a little more flour if dough is too sticky). Turn out onto a lightly floured surface and knead for 10 minutes or until smooth and elastic. Place dough in a oiled bowl and turn to coat, then cover with plastic wrap and leave in a draught-free place for 1-1½ hours or until nearly doubled in size.

Using existing markings on chocolate as a guide, break 16 squares from chocolate bars (you will have a few squares left over).

Knock down dough, then turn out onto a lightly floured surface and divide into 8 pieces. Using a rolling pin, roll out each piece until 8x15cm. Place a dough rectangle widthways in front of you and place 2 squares of chocolate in a single layer in the centre, then fold over one-third of dough to cover chocolate, brush folded piece of dough with egg white mixture, then fold remaining third of dough over first fold and press down gently. Repeat with remaining dough, chocolate, and egg white mixture. Sprinkle tops with a little extra caster sugar.

Place pain au chocolat on a greased oven tray and bake at 190C for 20-25 minutes or until golden. Serve hot or at room temperature with bowls of milky hot chocolate, if using, for breakfast or as a snack.

Makes 8

Chocolate buns

150g caster sugar

7g dried yeast

600g (4 cups) plain flour

30g cocoa

1 egg yolk

1 tablespoon vegetable oil

175g dark chocolate, chopped

Soft butter, for greasing

55g (¼ cup) caster sugar, extra

Ricotta, to serve

Place ¾ cup lukewarm water in a small bowl, stir in 1 teaspoon sugar, sprinkle over yeast and stand for 10 minutes or until mixture is foamy.

Sift remaining sugar, flour, cocoa and ½ teaspoon salt into a large bowl, make a well in the centre and pour in the yeast mixture, egg yolk, oil and 1 cup lukewarm water. Stir in chocolate and mix well.

Turn out onto a lightly floured surface and knead for 10 minutes or until smooth and elastic. Form dough into a ball, place in a greased bowl, turn to coat, then cover with plastic wrap and leave in a draught-free place for 1½-2 hours or until doubled in size.

Grease a 12-hole (⅓-cup-capacity) muffin tin. Knock down dough and divide into 12 even pieces, then lightly knead each piece and place in muffin tin. Cover with a clean towel and leave in a draught-free place for 1 hour or until doubled in size. Bake at 200C for 15 minutes or until well risen and hollow sounding when tapped. Turn out onto a wire rack to cool.

Combine extra sugar and 2 tablespoons water in a small saucepan and stir over low heat until sugar dissolves, then brush hot glaze over hot buns.

Serve buns warm or at room temperature with ricotta passed separately. Chocolate buns will keep in an airtight container for up to 2 days.

Makes 12

Rich chocolate tart

125g cold unsalted butter, chopped

1 tablespoon caster sugar

200g (1⅓ cups) plain flour

2 tablespoons Dutch-process cocoa

2 egg yolks

Double cream, optional, to serve

Filling

300g dark couverture chocolate, finely chopped

100ml double cream

125g unsalted butter, chopped

4 eggs

100g caster sugar

1 tablespoon golden syrup

Process butter, sugar, flour and cocoa in a food processor until mixture resembles coarse breadcrumbs. Add egg yolks and 1½ tablespoons iced water and process until pastry just comes together. Form pastry into a disc, wrap in plastic wrap and refrigerate for at least 30 minutes.

Roll out pastry on a lightly floured surface until 5mm thick and ease into a 3.5cm-deep 24cm tart tin with removable base, trimming edge. Line pastry with baking paper and fill with dried beans or rice, place tin on an oven tray and bake at 180C for 20 minutes, then remove paper and beans and bake for another 5 minutes or until pastry is dry. Cool.

For filling, combine chocolate, cream and butter in a heatproof bowl over a saucepan of simmering water and stir continuously until butter is melted and mixture is well combined, then remove bowl from heat and set aside. Using an electric mixer, whisk eggs, sugar and golden syrup until pale and creamy, then fold into chocolate mixture. Pour filling into tart shell and bake at 150C for 35-40 minutes or until just set. Cool tart to room temperature before serving with double cream, if using. Tart will keep, refrigerated, in an airtight container for up to 4 days.

Serves 8

Chocolate eclairs with crème de cassis cream

Alternatively, the cream can be flavoured with an orange or coffee-flavoured liqueur.

2 teaspoons caster sugar
60g unsalted butter, chopped
90g plain flour
2 eggs
Filling
300ml thickened cream
40g (¼ cup) icing sugar, sifted
1 tablespoon crème de cassis
Glaze
100g dark couverture chocolate, chopped
30g liquid glucose
2½ tablespoons thickened cream

Combine sugar, butter and ¾ teaspoon salt with 185ml cold water in a small saucepan and bring to the boil. Remove from heat, add all the flour at once and, using a wooden spoon, stir vigorously until mixture is smooth, then return mixture to a low heat and stir for 1-2 minutes or until mixture comes away from side of pan. Immediately transfer mixture to the bowl of an electric mixer and, with motor running, add eggs one at a time, beating well after each. Spoon mixture into a piping bag fitted with a 15mm plain nozzle and pipe 8cm lengths 3cm apart on baking paper-lined oven trays, cutting each length with a small knife. Bake at 220C for 15 minutes. Reduce oven temperature to 180C and bake for another 10 minutes. Turn off oven and cool pastries in oven with door slightly ajar.

For filling, using an electric mixer, whisk cream and icing sugar until soft peaks form, add liqueur and whisk until just combined. Using a serrated knife, cut pastries in half horizontally, taking care not to cut all the way through, then fill each with a little cream mixture.

For glaze, combine all ingredients in a heatproof bowl over a saucepan of simmering water and stir until well combined. Cool for 5 minutes, then spread a little glaze over the top of each eclair.

Place eclairs on a tray and refrigerate for 1 hour or until glaze is set. Unfilled pastries can be made a day ahead and stored in an airtight container. Filled eclairs are best served on day of making.

Makes about 25 small eclairs

Chocolate, pear and amaretti tart

200g (1⅓ cups) plain flour
55g (¼ cup) caster sugar
100g ground almonds
125g soft unsalted butter
1 egg
2 ripe packham or beurre bosc pears,
    peeled, quartered and cored
1 tablespoon caster sugar, extra
Icing sugar, optional, for dusting
Double cream, to serve

Filling

50g unsalted butter
1 tablespoon Dutch-process cocoa
1 egg
1 teaspoon vanilla extract
180g caster sugar
30g amaretti biscuits, crushed
50g (⅓ cup) plain flour

Sift together flour, sugar, ground almonds and ¼ teaspoon salt. Add butter and, using fingertips, rub into flour until mixture resembles breadcrumbs. Add egg combined with 1 tablespoon iced water, then, using a wooden spoon, stir until mixture almost comes together. Turn out dough onto a work surface and press together to form a disc, wrap in plastic wrap and refrigerate for 30 minutes. Roll out pastry on a lightly floured surface and line an 11x34cm rectangular tart tin with removable base.

Place pear quarters in a bowl, sprinkle with extra sugar and toss well to combine, then place in a row, widthways, in tart shell. Bake at 190C for 15 minutes or until pastry is light golden, remove from oven and cool for 5 minutes.

Meanwhile, for filling, combine butter and cocoa in a small saucepan and stir over low heat until butter melts. Using an electric mixer, whisk egg, vanilla and sugar until thick and creamy. Add cocoa mixture and amaretti biscuits and stir until well combined, then gently fold in flour. Pour mixture around pear quarters and bake at 190C for 40 minutes or until just set. Cool tart to room temperature (the filling will remain a little soft in the centre), then dust with icing sugar, if using, and serve with double cream passed separately.

Serves 8

Chocolate and hazelnut filo roll

5 sheets filo pastry

50g ground hazelnuts or almonds

2 tablespoons caster sugar

1 teaspoon ground cinnamon

125g unsalted butter, melted

Icing sugar, for dusting

Filling

100g hazelnuts, roasted,
  peeled and cooled

250g dark chocolate, chopped

1 tablespoon finely grated orange rind

For filling, process hazelnuts and chocolate in a food processor, using the pulse button, until coarsely chopped, then stir in orange rind.

Unroll filo pastry and cover with a slightly damp tea towel. Combine ground hazelnuts, sugar and cinnamon in a small bowl. Place a sheet of pastry on a work surface and brush with melted butter, then top with a second pastry sheet and brush with melted butter. Sprinkle one-third of the nut mixture over pastry, then top with another pastry sheet, brush with butter and sprinkle with another third of the nut mixture. Repeat with another layer of pastry, butter and remaining nut mixture. Top with final pastry sheet and brush with butter. Place the filling on the lowest third of the pastry layers, leaving a 2cm border. Tuck in edges, then, gently but firmly, roll pastry into a log shape and place, seam-side down, on a baking paper-lined oven tray. Brush roll with butter, then bake at 180C for 30-35 minutes, or until golden and firm. Transfer to a wire rack and cool to room temperature. Trim edges with a sharp knife, dust with icing sugar and cut into 2cm-thick slices. Serve warm or at room temperature.

Serves 6-8

Bitter chocolate tarts

200g (1⅓ cups) plain flour
2 tablespoons caster sugar
120g butter, chopped,
   plus extra, for greasing
Gold leaf, optional, to serve
Chocolate filling
150ml thickened cream
150g dark couverture chocolate,
   finely chopped
1 teaspoon tokay or brandy
2 egg yolks

Combine flour, sugar and a pinch of salt in a bowl, then, using fingertips, rub in butter until mixture just comes together. Turn out onto a lightly floured surface and knead gently until dough is smooth. Form dough into a disc, wrap in plastic wrap and refrigerate for 30 minutes.

Roll out dough on a lightly floured surface until 3mm thick. Using a 7.5cm fluted pastry cutter, cut out rounds. Press rounds into lightly greased tartlet trays, prick pastry with a fork, then freeze for 30 minutes. Bake at 180C for 12 minutes or until pastry is dry and just beginning to colour. Cool.

For chocolate filling, bring cream just to the boil in a small saucepan, then remove from heat. Add chopped chocolate and whisk until chocolate is melted and mixture is smooth. Cool chocolate mixture to room temperature, stirring occasionally, then whisk in alcohol and egg yolks. Spoon chocolate filling into cooled tart cases and refrigerate for 30 minutes or until just set.

Serve chocolate tarts topped with a small piece of gold leaf, if using. Tarts will keep, refrigerated, in an airtight container for up to 3 days.
Makes about 18 tarts

Chocolate almond fudge

250g unsalted butter, chopped
1½ cups milk
50g (½ cup) Dutch-process cocoa
1kg caster sugar
90g (¾ cup) chopped blanched almonds
1 teaspoon vanilla extract

Combine butter, milk, cocoa and sugar in a large heavy-based saucepan and stir over medium heat until sugar dissolves and mixture is smooth. Bring mixture to the boil and cook, uncovered, stirring occasionally, until mixture reaches 116C (soft-ball stage) on a sugar thermometer or until a small piece dropped into cold water forms a soft ball.

Remove mixture from heat and cool for 5 minutes, then, using a wooden spoon, beat for 2-3 minutes or until mixture is thick but still glossy. Stir in almonds and vanilla and mix until well combined. Pour mixture into a greased, shallow 18x26cm pan, smooth top and cool for 2 hours or until set.

To remove fudge from pan, run a knife around edge of pan and invert onto a chopping board, then cut fudge into 2.5cm squares. Fudge will keep, refrigerated, in an airtight container for up to 4 weeks.
Makes about 50 pieces

Chocolate madeleines

Soft butter, for greasing
100g unsalted butter, chopped
70g plain flour
25g (¼ cup) Dutch-process cocoa
40g (⅓ cup) ground almonds
3 eggs
110g (½ cup) caster sugar,
    plus extra, for dusting

Brush an 8cm-hole madeleine tin with soft butter and refrigerate until cold, then repeat process.

Melt chopped butter in a small saucepan until foamy and light brown, then remove from heat and strain through a fine sieve. Cool.

Sift together flour, cocoa, ground almonds and a pinch of salt.

Using an electric mixer, whisk eggs and sugar until mixture holds a trail. Add flour mixture and cooled butter and stir gently until well combined. Stand mixture for 10 minutes, then spoon level tablespoonfuls of mixture into holes of prepared tin and bake at 190C for 8-10 minutes. Carefully transfer madeleines, ridged-side up, onto a wire rack to cool. Repeat with remaining madeleine mixture, double-buttering and chilling madeleine tin again.

Serve madeleines dusted with a little extra caster sugar. Madeleines will keep in an airtight container for up to 3 days, or can be frozen for up to 1 month.

Makes about 20

Chocolate and honey matchsticks

500g dark couverture chocolate,
  coarsely chopped
150ml pouring cream
50g honey
2 thinly peeled strips of lemon rind
Dutch-process cocoa, for dusting

Process 300g chocolate in a food processor until finely chopped.

Combine cream, honey and lemon rind in a small saucepan and bring to the boil, then discard lemon rind. Pour hot cream mixture onto chocolate in food processor and process until chocolate is melted and mixture is thick. Transfer mixture to a bowl and stand at room temperature for 30 minutes or until thick enough to pipe. Spoon mixture into a piping bag fitted with a 7mm plain nozzle. Line 3 trays with baking paper, then, using a pencil, mark fourteen 28cm lines 3cm apart on the paper. Pipe chocolate in lines using pencil markings as a guide, then refrigerate for 1 hour.

Working with 1 tray at a time, slide a knife under chocolate strips to loosen them, then cut each strip into 4 and place in a large container, taking care not to stack matchsticks more than 3 deep. Cover and refrigerate overnight.

Melt remaining chocolate in a heatproof bowl over a saucepan of simmering water, then remove bowl from saucepan. Wearing latex gloves, coat your palm with a little chocolate and gently roll each matchstick in chocolate, then carefully place on a baking paper-lined tray and stand until set.

Dust chocolate matchsticks with cocoa. Matchsticks will keep, refrigerated, in an airtight container for up to 1 month.

Makes about 170

Orange chocolate-dipped almonds

150g dark couverture chocolate, finely chopped
¼ teaspoon pure orange oil
200g dry-roasted almonds
40g (¼ cup) icing sugar, sifted
40g Dutch-process cocoa, sifted

Melt chocolate in a heatproof bowl over a saucepan of simmering water and stir until smooth, then remove from heat. Add orange oil and stir well to combine. Using two forks, dip almonds, one at a time, in chocolate mixture, shaking gently to remove excess, then place on foil-lined oven trays. Stand chocolate almonds at room temperature until chocolate is just set (but not hard). Meanwhile, place icing sugar and cocoa in separate bowls and set aside. Toss half the almonds in icing sugar and half in cocoa, shaking away excess. Store almonds in an airtight container in a cool place for up to 2 weeks.
Makes about 135

Chocolate nut wafers

100g soft unsalted butter
55g (¼ cup) caster sugar
60g honey
2 egg whites
80g plain flour
200g dark couverture chocolate, coarsely chopped
150g (1 cup) hazelnuts, roasted, peeled and coarsely chopped
160g (1 cup) blanched almonds, roasted and coarsely chopped

Process butter, sugar, honey and egg whites in a food processor
for 5 minutes or until smooth and creamy. Transfer mixture to
a bowl and stir in flour until just combined.

Combine dark chocolate and nuts in a small bowl.

Line two 22.5x33cm oven trays with baking paper and thinly
spread one-quarter of the wafer batter over each tray, then
scatter each tray with one-quarter of the chocolate nut mixture.
Bake at 170C for 12-15 minutes or until golden. Remove from
oven and cool on trays. Repeat process with remaining wafer
batter and chocolate nut mixture.

To serve, break into large pieces. Wafers will keep in
an airtight container for up to 3 days.
Makes about 36

Chocolate snaps

50g unsalted butter, chopped, plus extra, for greasing
1½ tablespoons golden syrup
2 tablespoons brown sugar
2 tablespoons plain flour, sifted
2 tablespoons ground hazelnuts
175g dark chocolate, melted

Melt butter, golden syrup and sugar in a small saucepan over low heat, stirring until butter melts. Remove from heat, add flour and ground hazelnuts and mix well. Place ¼ teaspoonfuls of mixture 5cm apart on greased oven trays and bake at 160C for about 5 minutes or until golden. Remove and cool on trays for 2-3 minutes or until firm, then carefully remove with a spatula. Cool to room temperature on a wire rack.

Melt chocolate in a heatproof bowl over a saucepan of simmering water. Dip half of each snap in melted chocolate, allowing excess to drip off, then place on baking paper-lined oven trays until set.

Store chocolate snaps in an airtight container in a cool place for up to 2 days.

Makes about 40

Three chocolate truffles

All truffle recipes make 40. Truffles will keep, refrigerated, in an airtight container for up to 1 week. Bring to room temperature before serving.

Chocolate almond truffles

300g dark couverture chocolate, chopped
⅓ cup thickened cream
20g unsalted butter
130g blanched whole almonds,
   roasted and finely chopped
¼ teaspoon vanilla extract

Place chocolate, cream and butter in a heatproof bowl over a saucepan of simmering water and stir occasionally until smooth, then remove bowl from heat. Stir in 30g chopped almonds and vanilla until well combined, then cover and refrigerate for 1-2 hours or until firm enough to roll into balls.

Spread remaining almonds over a shallow tray, then, using your hands, roll teaspoonfuls of chocolate mixture into small balls and roll in chopped almonds until well coated. Place truffles on a baking paper-lined tray and refrigerate for at least 1 hour before serving.

Tia Maria truffles

300g dark couverture chocolate, chopped
⅓ cup thickened cream
2 tablespoons Tia Maria or Kahlúa
100g (1 cup) Dutch-process cocoa, sifted

Place chocolate and cream in a heatproof bowl over a saucepan of simmering water and stir occasionally until smooth, then remove bowl from heat and stir in liqueur. Cover and refrigerate for 1-2 hours or until firm enough to roll into balls. Spread cocoa over a shallow tray, then, using your hands, roll teaspoonfuls of chocolate mixture into small balls and roll in cocoa until well coated. Place truffles on a baking paper-lined tray and refrigerate for at least 1 hour before serving.

White chocolate and lemon truffles

300g white couverture chocolate, chopped
⅓ cup thickened cream
Few drops of vanilla extract
3 teaspoons finely grated lemon rind
90g (1 cup) desiccated coconut, toasted

Place chocolate and cream in a heatproof bowl over a saucepan of simmering water and stir occasionally until smooth, then remove bowl from heat and stir in vanilla and lemon rind. Cover and refrigerate for 1-2 hours or until firm enough to roll into balls. Spread coconut over a shallow tray, then, using your hands, roll teaspoonfuls of chocolate mixture into small balls and roll in coconut until well coated. Place truffles on baking paper-lined tray and refrigerate for at least 1 hour before serving.

Dessert hot chocolate

2½ cups pouring cream
3 teaspoons icing sugar, sifted
100g dark couverture chocolate, finely chopped
½ cup milk
½ cup thickened cream, softly whipped

Combine ½ cup cream and icing sugar in a bowl and whisk until firm peaks form.

Place chocolate, milk and remaining cream in a saucepan and stir over low-medium heat until chocolate melts and mixture is smooth and hot. Remove from heat and pour into warmed mugs. Top with spoonfuls of whipped cream and serve immediately.

Serves 4

White hot chocolate

650ml milk
1 tablespoon caster sugar
1 tablespoon Bailey's Irish Cream
150g white couverture chocolate, chopped
½ cup thickened cream, softly whipped
Dutch-process cocoa, for dusting

Place milk in a saucepan and bring almost to the boil, remove from heat, then stir in sugar and liqueur until sugar dissolves. Add chocolate and stir until chocolate melts and mixture is smooth. Pour chocolate mixture into warmed mugs, top with spoonfuls of whipped cream, dust with cocoa and serve immediately.

Serves 4

Dark chocolate crème anglaise

6 egg yolks
125g caster sugar
600ml milk
150g dark chocolate, chopped

Whisk egg yolks and sugar in a large bowl until mixture is thick and pale. Place milk in a large saucepan and bring almost to the boil, then gently whisk hot milk into egg yolk mixture until well combined. Return mixture to saucepan and stir continuously over low heat until mixture thickens enough to coat the back of a wooden spoon. Do not boil.

Transfer custard to a large bowl, add chocolate and stir until custard is smooth, strain, then cool to room temperature. Custard will keep refrigerated for up to 3 days.

Makes about 1 litre

Variations

White chocolate crème anglaise: Follow recipe for dark chocolate crème anglaise, substituting 150g chopped white couverture chocolate and adding 2 tablespoons kirsch or orange-flavoured liqueur.

Milk chocolate and ginger crème anglaise: Following recipe for dark chocolate crème anglaise, bring milk and 1 tablespoon grated ginger almost to the boil, then remove from heat and stand for 20 minutes. Continue as instructed, substituting 150g chopped milk couverture chocolate. Stir until custard is smooth, strain, then cool to room temperature.

AMARENA CHERRIES: a variety of sour cherry grown in Italy and cured in syrup. Unlike common glacé cherries, they retain their deep garnet colour and subtle cherry flavour.

AMARETTI BISCUITS: crunchy or soft small Italian-style macaroons based on ground almonds. The hard variety, which also contains ground apricot kernels and almond extract, was used in this book.

AMARETTO: almond-flavoured liqueur from Italy.

BAILEY'S IRISH CREAM: a blend of fresh cream, Irish spirits, Irish whiskey, cocoa and vanilla.

BAKING POWDER: a raising agent that is two parts cream of tartar to one part bicarbonate of soda (baking soda).

BITTERSWEET CHOCOLATE: chocolate with a high content of cocoa butter and cocoa liquor (known as cocoa solids) and a lower proportion of sugar, resulting in a characteristic bitter/sweet flavour. We used a chocolate with 70 per cent cocoa solids which is available from supermarkets.

BOYAJIAN PURE ORANGE OIL: citrus oil cold pressed from the rind of oranges; 220 oranges are required to produce a 150ml/5oz bottle. Available from specialty food stores and delicatessens.

BUTTER: use salted or unsalted (sweet) butter as directed (125g is equal to one stick of butter).

CASTER SUGAR: superfine or finely granulated table sugar.

CHOCOLAT ROYAL: chocolate-flavoured liqueur.

COCOA POWDER: made by removing most of the cocoa butter from cocoa solids, leaving behind a solid, dry mass which is then ground into a powder. The taste can be bitter and the colour a dusty brown. See also *Dutch-process cocoa*.

COINTREAU: orange-flavoured liqueur from France.

CORNFLOUR: also known as cornstarch; used as a thickening agent in cooking.

COUVERTURE CHOCOLATE: top-quality dark or milk chocolate with a high percentage of cocoa butter and cocoa liquor (known as cocoa solids) that range from 50 to 99 per cent. The higher the cocoa content the more intense and bitter the chocolate flavour. It is sold in large 1-5kg blocks from specialty food stores, but is also available from some delicatessens repackaged in smaller weights. Couverture chocolate is more viscous than plain chocolate and, when tempered (a process that stabilises the chocolate by heating, then cooling), is ideal for coating, giving a long-lasting high gloss and crisp finish. Available from delicatessens and specialty food stores.

CREME DE CASSIS: blackcurrant-flavoured liqueur.

DUTCH-PROCESS COCOA: 'dutching' is a method of alkalising cocoa. An alkali is added during processing, neutralising the astringent quality of the cocoa and giving it a rich, dark colour and smoother, more rounded flavour. Available from delicatessens and specialty food stores.

GERANIUM WATER: concentrated aromatic flavouring from Tunisia; if unavailable, substitute rose or orange flower water.

GLACE CITRON: made from a citrus fruit resembling a large rough-skinned lemon. Available from delicatessens and specialty food stores.

GLACE CLEMENTINE: made from a hybrid of the mandarin and the seville orange. Available from delicatessens and specialty food stores.

GOLD LEAF: available from cake decorator or art supply stores.

GRAND MARNIER: orange-flavoured liqueur based on cognac brandy.

ICING SUGAR: also known as powdered sugar or confectioner's sugar.

KAHLUA: coffee-flavoured liqueur from Mexico.

KIRSCH: a clear fruit brandy distilled from cherries.

LIQUEUR MUSCAT: a dark sweet dessert wine unique to Australia. Made from a dark-skinned strain of grapes called muscat blanc à petits grains, that are semi-dried on the vine, partially fermented, then fortified with grape spirit and aged in wooden casks. If unavailable, substitute sweet sherry or port.

LIQUID GLUCOSE: used in baking and confectionery making as a sweetener, as it does not crystallise easily. Available from health food stores.

MALIBU: coconut-flavoured rum.

MASCARPONE: a fresh, smooth, unripened, triple cream cheese with a rich, slightly acidic, taste.

MEXICAN-STYLE CHOCOLATE: a sweet chocolate flavoured with cinnamon, Ibarra is the most common brand. If unavailable, for the Mexican Chocolate Pots on page 15, substitute 200g dark chocolate and add 40g caster sugar and ½ teaspoon ground cinnamon.

OUZO: aniseed-flavoured liqueur from Greece.

PLAIN CHOCOLATE: plain dark chocolate consists of chocolate liquor mixed with powdered sugar and small quantities of cocoa butter. It is usually sold for eating and has a mild flavour.

SAMBUCA: anise-flavoured liqueur from Italy.

TIA MARIA: coffee-flavoured liqueur from Jamaica.

WHITE CHOCOLATE: strictly speaking, not chocolate as it contains no cocoa solids, but is a mixture of cocoa butter, milk solids, sugar and flavouring. The best white chocolate for cooking is white couverture chocolate which contains high proportions of the aforementioned ingredients; many white chocolates are just for eating and contain other fats and additions that make them hard to melt and use in cooking.

MELT CHOCOLATE in a microwave oven or in a bowl over simmering water. Do not melt over too high a heat or over direct heat by itself as it will become grainy, coarse and unusable. To melt over direct heat, it must be combined with a liquid, such as milk or cream. **To melt chocolate on a stove:** place chopped chocolate in a heatproof bowl large enough to sit tightly over a saucepan one-third filled with just simmering water, ensuring the base of the bowl does not touch the water, then stir until chocolate melts. It is important that no water or steam comes into contact with the chocolate or it will become grainy. **To melt chocolate in a microwave oven:** place chocolate in a glass or ceramic bowl and microwave, uncovered, on 50 per cent or medium power at 30-60 second intervals, depending on the quantity of chocolate used, stirring after each interval (important as chocolate does not lose its shape in the microwave), until it is melted and smooth.

CHOP CHOCOLATE by using a sharp serrated knife. Alternatively process broken pieces in a food processor using the pulse button.

STORE CHOCOLATE in a cool, dry place away from direct sunlight. Wrap opened chocolate in foil or baking paper, then in plastic wrap and store in an airtight container. Humidity and temperature changes can cause chocolate to develop a fat bloom (sugar crystals rise to surface causing a pitted look). In this state it can still be used for cooking but is not suitable for confectionery making, coating or decorating.

measures

One Australian metric measuring cup holds approximately 250ml, one Australian metric tablespoon holds 20ml, one Australian metric teaspoon holds 5ml. The difference between one country's measuring cups and another's is within a two- or three-teaspoon variance. North America, New Zealand and the United Kingdom use a 15ml tablespoon.

All cup and spoon measurements are level.

We use large eggs with an average weight of 60g.

Unless specified, all fruit is medium sized.

DRY MEASURES

metric	imperial
15g	½oz
30g	1oz
60g	2oz
90g	3oz
125g	4oz (¼lb)
155g	5oz
185g	6oz
220g	7oz
250g	8oz (½lb)
280g	9oz
315g	10oz
345g	11oz
375g	12oz (¾lb)
410g	13oz
440g	14oz
470g	15oz
500g	16oz (1lb)
750g	24oz (1½lb)
1kg	32oz (2lb)

LIQUID MEASURES

metric	imperial
30ml	1 fluid oz
60ml	2 fluid oz
100ml	3 fluid oz
125ml	4 fluid oz
150ml	5 fluid oz (¼ pint/1 gill)
190ml	6 fluid oz
250ml	8 fluid oz
300ml	10 fluid oz (½ pint)
500ml	16 fluid oz
600ml	20 fluid oz (1 pint)
1000ml (1 litre)	1¾ pints

LENGTH MEASURES

metric	imperial
3mm	⅛in
6mm	¼in
1cm	½in
2cm	¾in
2.5cm	1in
5cm	2in
6cm	2½in
8cm	3in
10cm	4in
13cm	5in
15cm	6in
18cm	7in
20cm	8in
23cm	9in
25cm	10in
28cm	11in
30cm	12in (1ft)

OVEN TEMPERATURES

These oven temperatures are only a guide. Always check the manufacturer's manual.

	°C (Celsius)	°F (Fahrenheit)	Gas Mark
Very slow	120	250	1
Slow	150	300	2
Moderately slow	160	325	3
Moderate	180-190	350-375	4
Moderately hot	200-210	400-425	5
Hot	220-230	450-475	6
Very hot	240-250	500-525	7